M000249280

Heinemann
First
Encyclopedia

Volume 5
Hom-Leo

Heinemann Library
Chicago, Illinois

Series Editors: Rebecca and Stephen Vickers
Author Team: Rob Alcraft, Catherine Chambers, Jim Drake,
Fred Martin, Angela Royston, Jane Shuter, Roger Thomas,
Rebecca Vickers, Stephen Vickers

Photo research by Katharine Smith
Designed and Typeset by Gecko Ltd
Printed in Hong Kong, China

03 02 01 00
10 9 8 7 6 5 4 3 2

Library of Congress Cataloging-in-Publication Data

Heinemann first encyclopedia.
     p.   cm.
    Summary: A ten-volume encyclopedia covering animals, plants,
countries, transportation, science, ancient civilizations, and world
history.
    ISBN 1-57572-741-2 (lib. bdg.)
    1. Children's encyclopedias and dictionaries. [1. Encyclopedias
and dictionaries.] I. Heinemann Library (Firm)
AG5.H45   1998
031—dc21   98-20016
                                     CIP
                                     AC

Acknowledgments

Cover: The cover illustration is of a male specimen of Ornithoptera goliath, commonly called the Goliath Birdwing. Special thanks to
Dr. George C. McGavin and the Hope Entomological Collections, Oxford University Museum of Natural History; J. Allan Cash Ltd.
pp. 4, 10, 12, 13, 14, 15, 20, 21, 22, 24 top, 26, 29, 30, 33, 34 top, 36, 40, 42; Ancient Art and Architecture, p. 23; Breslich and Foss,
p. 38; Bridgeman Art Library, p. 47 bottom; BBC Natural History Unit/Brian Lightfoot p. 17 top; Bruce Coleman/Trevor Barrett, p.
45 top; Hulton Deutsch, pp. 7 top, 16; The Hutchison Library, p. 5; T.E. Clarke, p. 27; Chris Johnson, p. 46; Lisa Taylor, p. 34
bottom; Jazz Photo Library/Christian Him, p. 31 top; Peter Newark, p. 47 top; Oxford Scientific Film, p. 17 bottom; Alan and
Sandy Carey, p. 28 bottom; Kenneth Day, p. 39 top; Richard Day, p. 9 bottom; Douglas Faulkner, p. 25 top; MPL Fogden, p. 19;
Frances Furlong, p. 48 top; Frank Huber, p. 25 bottom; Breck Kent, p. 32 top; Renee Lynn, p. 28 top; Tom McHugh, p. 37 top; T.C.
Nature, p. 9 top; Peter Parks, p. 32 bottom; Ralph Rheinhold, p. 6 top; Tui de Roy, p. 37 bottom; Kjell Sandved, p. 39 bottom;
Richard Shiell, p. 41 bottom; Victoria Stone, p. 48 bottom; Philip Tull, p. 6 bottom; Redferns, p. 31 bottom; Science Photo
Library/NASA, pp. 11 bottom, 44 top; Philippe Plailly, p. 44 bottom; Tony Stone Worldwide/Cameron Davidson, p. 11 top; Mary
Kate Denny, p. 43; Trip, p. 24 bottom; Zefa, p. 7 bottom.

Every effort has been made to contact copyright holders of any material
reproduced in this book. Any omissions will be rectified in subsequent
printings if notice is given to the Publisher.

Welcome to
Heinemann First Encyclopedia

What is an encyclopedia?

An encyclopedia is an information book. It gives the most important facts about many different subjects. This encyclopedia has been written for children who are using an encyclopedia for the first time. It covers many of the subjects from school and others you may find interesting.

What is in this encyclopedia?

In this encyclopedia, each topic is called an *entry*. There is one page of information for every entry. The entries in this encyclopedia explain

- animals
- plants
- dinosaurs
- countries
- geography
- history
- world religions
- music
- art
- transportation
- science
- technology

How to use this encyclopedia

This encyclopedia has eleven books called *volumes*. The first ten volumes contain entries. The entries are all in alphabetical order. This means that Volume 1 starts with entries that begin with the letter *A* and Volume 10 ends with entries that begin with the letter *Z*. Volume 11 is the index volume. It also has interesting information about American history.

Here are two entries that show you what you can find on a page:

The "see also" line tells you where to find other related information.

This is the letter that the entry starts with.

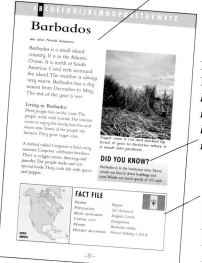

Fact boxes give you details about the topic.

Did You Know? boxes have fun or interesting bits of information.

The Fact File tells you important facts and figures.

Home

see also: Architecture

A home is where someone lives. It is also a place where someone keeps what they own. Many animals also have homes where they sleep and care for their young. About half of the people in the world live in homes in towns and cities. The other half lives in the country.

This house in Ethiopia is built with thatch. This is a traditional way of building houses in parts of Africa.

Types of homes

A person's home can be a house, a tent, a houseboat, or an apartment. Most homes protect people from the weather. A house in a hot country might be painted white. The color white reflects the sun. The color white helps homes stay cool.

Families and homes

Some homes hold a small family. Some homes hold a big family. A family in Africa might have parents, children, aunts, uncles, cousins, and grandparents living together. Their homes are huts inside a walled area. The walled area is called a compound.

Some people live in cities where there is not much space. Lots of homes can be built in a tall apartment building. These apartment buildings are in New York City.

DID YOU KNOW?

People called *nomads* move their homes from place to place. They live in tents or trailers. Nomads take their homes with them when they move.

Honduras

see also: North America

Honduras is a country in Central America. There are many mountains and river valleys. There is a long coast in the north. There is a short coast in the south. The climate is hot and wet. It is cooler in the mountains.

Living in Honduras

Most of the people live in the mountain valleys and on the coast. Most Hondurans work on farms and plantations. Bananas and coffee are grown to be sold to other countries. Farmers also grow corn. Hondurans eat bananas, coconuts, and shellfish. Tortillas are eaten every day.

The music in Honduras is a mixture of Spanish and local Native American styles. A special style of local dancing and singing is called *garífuna*.

These houses on Bay Island are built on stilts. There are wooden walkways between the houses.

DID YOU KNOW?

Honduras gets its name from the Spanish word that means "depths." This is because the Caribbean Sea off the north coast of Honduras is very deep.

NORTH AMERICA

FACT FILE

PEOPLE	Hondurans
POPULATION	about 6 million
MAIN LANGUAGES	Spanish, Native American
CAPITAL CITY	Tegucigalpa
MONEY	Lempira
HIGHEST MOUNTAIN	Mount Celaque–9,273
LONGEST RIVER	Patuca River–199 miles

Horse

see also: Mammal, Transportation

A horse is a large mammal. Some horses can run fast. Other horses pull heavy loads. Horses carried people and goods from place to place before trains and cars were invented. Today many people ride horses for pleasure.

HORSE FACTS

NUMBER OF	
KINDS	about 100
COLOR.	shades of brown, black, gray, white
HEIGHT.	up to 6 feet
WEIGHT	up to 2,600 lbs.
STATUS.	common
LIFE SPAN	usually 20 to 30 years
ENEMIES	mountain lions, wolves

Horse families

An adult male horse is called a stallion. An adult female horse is called a mare. A female horse usually has one baby at a time. The baby is called a foal. A young female horse is called a filly. A young male horse is called a colt. Some horses live in the wild. They live in groups called herds.

large eyes; one eye can look forward, while the other eye looks to the rear

long tail to flick away flies

an Arabian horse

long, strong legs to run fast or to pull heavy loads

hard hoofs to protect the foot

PLANT EATER

A large horse can eat up to 57 pounds of grass or oats and bran every day.

A mare feeds her foal her milk.

Hovercraft

see also: Transportation

A hovercraft is a type of transportation. It floats on a cushion of air. Hovercraft can move very quickly over land or water.

The first hovercraft

The first hovercraft was built in 1959 by a British engineer. It was a small machine. It carried two people. A large fan pushed air down. The air went under the machine. The air made a cushion of air. The machine floated on this cushion. A special skirt was added to keep the air in place under the machine. Later, powerful jet engines were added. Now hovercraft are large and fast.

This is the British engineer, Christopher Cockerell, testing his hovercraft.

How we use hovercraft

Large hovercraft carry people and cars. They are fast because they move above the water. They do not push through water like ships. They also travel quickly over sand and ice, but mostly they travel over water. Hovercraft are used all over the world for short journeys. Hovercraft engines need cleaning often, so they cannot travel long distances. Hovercraft use a lot of expensive fuel.

This large hovercraft carries passengers between England and France.

Human Body

see also: Blood, Heart, Lung

The human body is made up of many parts. All the parts work together.

The human machine

Each of the organs in the human body acts as part of a system. These systems keep the body working. The heart, arteries, and veins are part of the circulatory system. They move the blood around the body. The stomach and intestines are part of the digestive system. They process the food that a person eats. The lungs are part of the respiratory system. They are used for breathing in oxygen and breathing out carbon dioxide.

Healthy systems

All the systems must help each other for a person to be healthy. For example, the muscles in the arm help a person pick up food. Muscles in the jaw help to chew the food. Then the digestive system gets the food. It takes the important things called nutrients out of the food. The nutrients go into the circulatory system. The circulatory system carries the nutrients to the areas in the body where the nutrients are needed.

DID YOU KNOW?

Nearly three-fourths of the human body is made up of water.

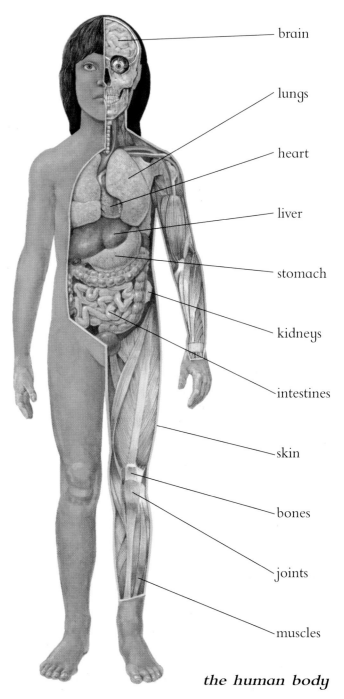

brain

lungs

heart

liver

stomach

kidneys

intestines

skin

bones

joints

muscles

the human body

Hummingbird

see also: Bird, Migration

A hummingbird is a small bird. It flaps its wings very fast. It can hover in one place. It can even fly backwards. Hummingbirds are found only in North and South America. Many hummingbirds migrate to warmer places for the winter. The bee hummingbird is the smallest bird in the world.

Hummingbird families

The male hummingbird has a special flying display. He does this to attract the female. The female makes a nest from lichens, bark, and spiders' webs. Then she lays two eggs. When the eggs hatch, she looks after the babies by herself. She feeds them nectar and insects.

colors to blend
with flowers

*an Anna's
hummingbird*

HUMMINGBIRD FACTS

NUMBER OF KINDS	334
COLOR	mostly bright colors
LENGTH	2 to 6 inches
WEIGHT	much less than an ounce
STATUS	common
LIFE SPAN	about 5 years
ENEMIES	dragonflies, spiders, frogs, people

strong muscles to
move wings very
fast

long beak
to sip nectar

This female ruby-throated
hummingbird covered her nest
with mossy-looking lichen.

PLANT AND INSECT EATER

A hummingbird drinks nectar from flowers. It also eats small insects.

Hungary

see also: Europe

Hungary is a country in central Europe. Most of the country is lowlands. Many crops grow well in the lowlands. Some mountains are in the northeast. Winters are cold. Summers are hot.

Living in Hungary

More than half of the people live in large towns and cities. The factories make steel, iron, electrical goods, and food products.

Farmers in the rural areas grow grapes, corn, potatoes, and sugar beets. Some people raise sheep and beef cattle. The most famous Hungarian dish is a beef stew called *goulash*. It is made with beef, a spice called paprika, and sour cream.

Tourists visit Hungary. More people visit Hungary each year than the number of people who live there.

Budapest is divided into two parts by the Danube River.

DID YOU KNOW?

The city of Budapest used to be two cities. The cities were on opposite sides of a river. Now bridges link Buda and Pest.

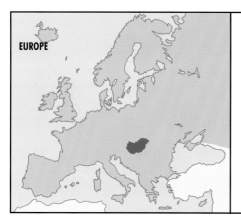

EUROPE

FACT FILE

PEOPLE	Hungarians
POPULATION	about 10 million
MAIN LANGUAGE	Magyar
CAPITAL CITY	Budapest
MONEY	Forint
HIGHEST MOUNTAIN	Kékes–3,330 feet
LONGEST RIVER	Tisza River–800 miles

Hurricane

see also: Tornado, Weather

A hurricane is a very strong storm. Hurricanes have wind speeds of at least 75 miles per hour. A hurricane can blow down trees. It can damage buildings. It can cause huge waves in the sea. Hurricanes in the Pacific Ocean are called *typhoons.*

This damage in North Carolina was caused by Hurricane Fran in 1996.

How hurricanes start
Hurricanes begin when warm air rises over a warm ocean or sea. More air moves in under the rising air. The air starts spinning around a center point. This center point is called the *eye of the hurricane.*

People and hurricanes
People can help themselves be safer during a hurricane. They can use boards to cover glass windows in their homes and shops. They can go to a hurricane shelter. Sometimes people move away from the area until the hurricane is over.

DID YOU KNOW?

Hurricanes are named in alphabetical order. The first hurricane of the year is given a name starting with the letter *A.* The next hurricane is given a name starting with *B.*

This picture of Hurricane Fran was taken from a satellite. The eye of the hurricane can be clearly seen.

Iceland

see also: Europe, Island

Iceland is an island country. It is northwest of Europe. The Atlantic Ocean is south of Iceland. The Arctic Ocean is to the north. Iceland has many volcanoes and glaciers.

DID YOU KNOW?

There is a warm ocean current called the Gulf Stream. It makes Iceland warmer in the winter than some countries in northern Europe.

Fishing is important to Iceland. The fish are sold to many other countries.

Living in Iceland

Nearly all Icelanders live in towns and cities. Some homes are heated with water from underground hot springs. The hot water is also used to warm greenhouses. Fruit and vegetables are grown in the greenhouses. The hot springs often squirt out high fountains of boiling water. These fountains are called *geysers*.

The most important jobs in Iceland are fishing and making food products from fish. There is not much farming. The soil isn't good enough to grow many crops. Sheep and cattle graze in the countryside.

Music is very important in Iceland. Almost everyone plays an instrument.

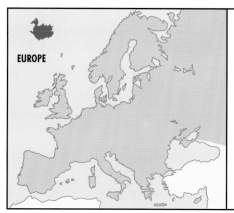

EUROPE

FACT FILE

PEOPLE	Icelanders
POPULATION	266 thousand
MAIN LANGUAGE	Icelandic
CAPITAL CITY	Reykjavík
MONEY	Icelandic króna
HIGHEST MOUNTAIN	Hvannadalsmukár–6,955 feet
LONGEST RIVER	Thjors River–143 miles

Incas

see also: Aztecs, Maya,
South America

The Incas were a native people in South America. They ruled part of what is now Chile, Ecuador, and Peru. They ruled about 500 years ago. The Incas began as a small group in about A.D. 1100. They took over more and more land and people. By 1525, they ruled about 10 million people.

What were the Incas like?

The Incas had a king. He was treated like a god. There were priests, warriors, traders, and other people who were mostly farmers. The Incas believed that many gods and goddesses controlled the world. The Incas prayed to the gods. They gave them presents to keep them happy. Sometimes Incas killed animals and people to give to the gods.

For what are the Incas known?

The Incas are remembered for their beautiful gold jewelry. They are known for their stone roads, cities, and temples. They had a way of keeping numbers on knotted string. The strings were called *quipu*.

KEY DATES

1100.....first Incas settle in the Cuzco Valley
1350.....Incas begin to take over more land
1439.....city of Cuzco is rebuilt as a capital city
1525.....Inca empire splits into two when its ruler dies
1532.....Spanish arrive and conquer the Incas

What happened to the Incas?

The Inca lands were split between two rulers. Then the Spanish arrived. Their powerful guns and cannons defeated the Incas.

The Inca city of Machu Picchu is now a ruin.

India

see also: Asia

India is a country in south Asia. The highest land is the Himalaya Mountains in the north. The Ganges River flows through a wide valley. There are cool, dry winds for part of the year. There are warm, wet winds for the other part of the year.

Living in India

India has the second most people of any country in the world. Three-fourths of the people live in villages. Most people work on farms. They grow rice. Calcutta and Bombay are big, crowded cities. There are factories in the cities.

The Ganges River is holy to Hindus. People use it to bathe. Ashes of the dead are scattered into it.

DID YOU KNOW?

The world religions of Buddhism, Hinduism, and Sikhism all began in India.

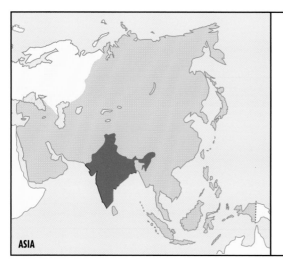

ASIA

FACT FILE

PEOPLE...................Indians

POPULATION...........over 1 billion

MAIN LANGUAGES... Hindi, English

CAPITAL CITY......... New Delhi

LARGEST CITY.........Bombay

MONEY...................Rupee

HIGHEST MOUNTAIN .... Kanchenjunga–28,208 feet

LONGEST RIVER.......Ganges River–1,558 miles

Indonesia

see also: Asia

Indonesia is a country in Asia. It has thousands of islands. There are mountains and active volcanoes on most of the islands. More than half of Indonesia is rainforest. The climate is mostly hot and very wet.

Living in Indonesia

About half of the people work in farming. Farmers cut steps into steep hillsides to make narrow fields. They grow rice. There are many new factories in Indonesia. Shoes, clothes, and other goods are made in the factories. These products are sold all over the world.

There are hundreds of different groups of people in Indonesia. The groups speak different languages. They have different customs.

These village houses in Indonesia are built on stilts to keep cool and dry.

DID YOU KNOW?

The Komodo dragon is the largest lizard in the world. It is found only in Indonesia. It is an endangered species.

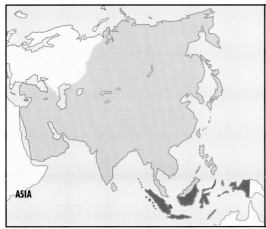

ASIA

FACT FILE

PEOPLE . . . . Indonesians

POPULATION . . . . about 210 million

MAIN LANGUAGE . . . Bahasa Indonesia

CAPITAL CITY . . . . Jakarta

MONEY . . . . Rupiah

HIGHEST
MOUNTAIN . . . . Puncak Jaya—16,505 feet

LONGEST RIVER . . . . Kapuas River—700 miles

Industrial Revolution

see also: United Kingdom

An industrial revolution is when factory machines begin to make things quickly. Many people begin to work in factories. Before an industrial revolution, people made things by hand. Most of the people were farmers.

The first industrial revolution

The first industrial revolution began in Britain in about 1750. Machines were invented that could spin and weave cloth quickly. The first machines were powered by water or operated by people. Then machines were driven by steam power. Coal was burned to make the steam.

KEY DATES

Different countries had industrial revolutions at different times in their histories.

1750s	Britain becomes industrialized.
1850s	Belgium, France, Germany, and the U.S.A. become industrialized.
1880s	Sweden and Japan become industrialized.
1900s	Russia and China become industrialized.
1950s	Parts of South America, Asia, and Africa become industrialized.

The revolution spreads

Other countries found out how Britain made things with machines. They copied these machines. They made the machines better. They had their own industrial revolutions.

These machines were used to spin cotton during the industrial revolution in Britain.

Insect

see also: Animals, Invertebrate, Metamorphosis

An insect is a small invertebrate. It has six legs. It has a hard covering around its body. Insects are common everywhere. They are on land, in the air, and in water.

Insect families

Most insects hatch from eggs that are laid by an adult female. A young insect is called a larva. The larva can look very different from the adult. The larva becomes a pupa. The pupa changes into an adult insect. The body of an adult insect has three parts. The three parts are the head, thorax, and abdomen. Some insects live together in groups called communities. Other insects live alone.

PLANT, INSECT, AND MEAT EATER

Some insects feed on plants. Others eat other animals. An insect either chews or sucks its food.

INSECT FACTS

NUMBER OF	
KINDS	more than 10 million
COLOR	often black, brown, or green
LENGTH	up to 4 inches
LIFE SPAN	usually less than a year
ENEMIES	birds, spiders, snakes, other animals, people

The green tiger beetle looks just like a green leaf. This helps it hide.

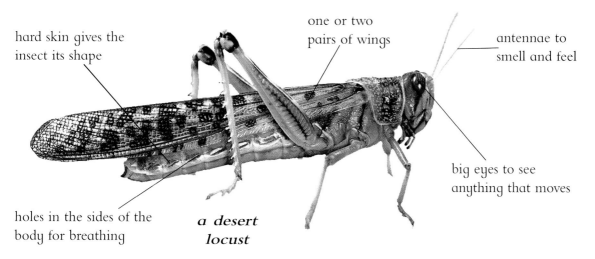

hard skin gives the insect its shape

one or two pairs of wings

antennae to smell and feel

big eyes to see anything that moves

holes in the sides of the body for breathing

a desert locust

Internet

see also: Communication, Computer, Telephone

The Internet is a way of connecting computers together. Computers anywhere in the world can send and receive information using the Internet. The World Wide Web is part of the Internet.

DID YOU KNOW?

E-mail is the short name for electronic mail. E-mail can be used just like mailing a letter. E-mail on the Internet sends messages between computers.

How does the Internet work?

The Internet started with a few powerful computers. The computers were connected. They could pass information to each other very quickly.

Now, personal computers (PCs) can be connected to the Internet using a modem. The modem helps to send messages along telephone lines. The messages go to a service provider. The service provider has a powerful computer. This computer passes the messages along to other computers.

Companies, organizations, and individual people can put information on web sites or home pages. The information can be about anything. Computers everywhere can get this information through the Internet.

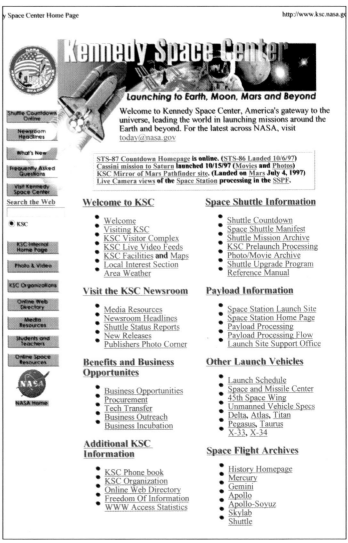

The Kennedy Space Center web site gives up-to-date information about the United States space program.

Invertebrate

see also: Crustacean, Insect, Mollusk, Vertebrate

An invertebrate is an animal that has no bones inside its body. Worms, jellyfish, snails, crabs, and insects are all invertebrates. Invertebrates are found everywhere in the world.

PLANT, INSECT, AND MEAT EATER

Different invertebrates eat different kinds of plants or animals. The shape of an invertebrate's mouth and body helps it to catch and eat the kind of food it likes.

Invertebrate families

Most invertebrates have several stages in their lives. A young invertebrate hatches out of an egg. It might not look like the adult. Most invertebrates are male or female. Some are both male and female at the same time.

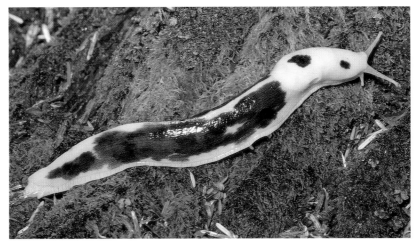

This is a banana slug. This invertebrate has no shell or hard covering to protect its soft body.

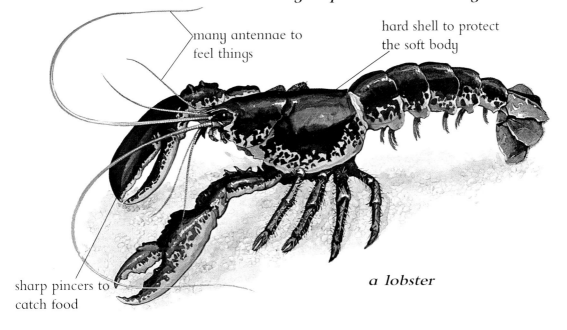

many antennae to feel things

hard shell to protect the soft body

sharp pincers to catch food

a lobster

Iran

see also: Asia, Islam

Iran is a country in southwest Asia. Most of the land is high and flat. There are mountains in the west. Winters in Iran are cold. Summers are much hotter. It rains in the north. The rest of Iran gets very little rain.

Living in Iran

About one third of the people are farmers. They grow rice and vegetables. Crops have to be watered because there is very little rain.

There are many oilfields in Iran. Most of the oil is sold to other countries. Some people work in factories that make the oil into chemicals.

Some Iranians still live the same way that their ancestors lived hundreds of years ago. They move with herds of sheep and goats to new grazing areas. These people are called nomads.

Most Iranians are followers of Islam. They follow strict laws about how to dress and what to eat and drink.

This prayer tower is on a mosque in the city of Isfahan. It is decorated with mosaic tiles. It is from here that people are called to pray five times a day.

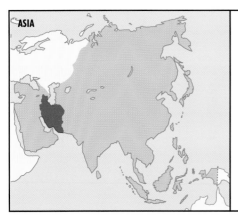

ASIA

FACT FILE

PEOPLE........................Iranians

POPULATION................ about 66 million

MAIN LANGUAGE..........Farsi (Persian)

CAPITAL CITY...............Tehran

MONEY.......................Rial

HIGHEST MOUNTAIN.... Damavand—18,392 feet

LONGEST RIVER .... Karun River—450 miles

Iraq

see also: Asia

Iraq is a country in southwest Asia. The Tigris and Euphrates Rivers flow through the middle of Iraq. They flow through flat land. The rivers make marshland as they flow south. There are mountains in the north. Most land in the west is desert. It is wettest in the north.

Living in Iraq

There is good farmland in the Tigris and Euphrates river valleys. About one-third of the people are farmers. They grow vegetables and grain. They raise cattle and goats. There are oilfields in Iraq. Some of the oil is sold to other countries.

During the 1980s, Iraq fought a war with Iran. This war ended in 1990. Then Iraq took over the country of Kuwait. This started the Gulf War. Many countries and the United Nations moved in to help Kuwait. Iraq lost this war.

Street vendors sell nuts outside the Golden Mosques in the city of Karbala.

DID YOU KNOW?

A people called Marsh Arabs live in southern Iraq. They live in floating raft houses made of reeds. There are few Marsh Arabs now because the marshes are being drained.

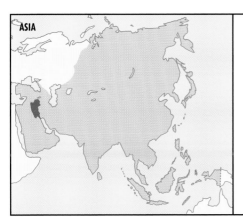

ASIA

FACT FILE

PEOPLE...................... Iraqis

POPULATION............... about 22 million

MAIN LANGUAGE......... Arabic

CAPITAL CITY.............. Baghdad

MONEY...................... Iraqi dinar

HIGHEST MOUNTAIN... Huji Ibrahim–11,815 feet

LONGEST RIVER.......... Euphrates River–1,677 miles

Ireland

see also: Europe,
Northern Ireland

The Republic of Ireland is a country. It is most of an island in western Europe. The center of Ireland is lowland. There are mountains in the far north and the southwest. The weather is usually mild and wet in winter. It is cool and wet in summer.

Living in Ireland

More than half of the people live in towns and cities. The rest of the people live on farms or in small country towns. More than half of the land is used for grazing cattle. Irish cheese and butter are sold to other countries.

Irish dancing and music are known around the world. Most people in Ireland are Roman Catholic. Two popular sports are Gaelic football and hurling.

Tourists come to Ireland to see the country. Many visit Blarney Castle. They kiss the Blarney stone in the castle wall. A legend says that kissing it will give you the gift of charming people with what you say.

DID YOU KNOW?

St. Patrick's Day is March 17. It is the country's main festival. There is a legend that St. Patrick drove all the snakes out of Ireland about 1,500 years ago.

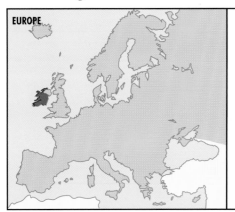

EUROPE

FACT FILE

PEOPLE........................Irish

POPULATION.............. about 3 million

MAIN LANGUAGES....... English, Irish Gaelic

CAPITAL CITY.............Dublin

MONEY......................Euro

HIGHEST MOUNTAIN... Carrantuohill–3,417 feet

LONGEST RIVER...........Shannon River–220 miles

Iron Age

see also: Bronze Age, Stone Age

The Iron Age is the time in a country's history when tools and weapons are made from iron. Before this time, tools were made from stone or bronze. People around the world discovered how to make weapons and tools from iron at different times. First, people had to learn how to get iron out of rocks. Then they had to learn how to make things from the iron.

Why was iron important?

Iron is easier to heat than bronze. It does not melt as quickly. It is easier to shape while it is soft. Tools and weapons made from iron are sharper and stronger than those made from bronze.

KEY DATES

4000 B.C.	People in the Middle East begin to use iron from meteoric rocks.
1500 B.C.	People in the Middle East begin to get iron out of rocks by heating the rocks.
1000 B.C.	People in India and Greece begin to use iron.
800 B.C.	People in Europe begin to use iron.
400 B.C.	People in China begin to use iron.
A.D.1750s	People begin to use steel.

What came next?

Iron was used for tools and machines until the 1750s. Then people found out that blowing oxygen over very hot iron makes a strong metal. This metal is called steel. People began making things with steel.

This Iron Age spearhead was found in France. It fit onto a wooden shaft. It is about 2,500 years old.

Islam

Islam is a world religion. Its followers are called *Muslims*. The religion started in Arabia in the Middle East. It was begun by Mohammed in A.D. 622.

Beliefs and teachings

Muslims follow the teachings of their holy book. The holy book is the Koran. They believe the Koran is the word of God. The word of God was given to Mohammed by the archangel Gabriel.

One of the teachings of Islam is that there is only one God and Mohammed is His Prophet. All Muslims must say they believe in God. They must pray and fast, or not eat, at certain times. They must give to the poor. They must go on a journey called a pilgrimage to Mecca. Mecca is the city in Saudi Arabia where Mohammed was born.

Islam today

There are now about one billion Muslims living all over the world. Most Muslims live in the Middle East, Africa, and Asia.

DID YOU KNOW?

The Koran is written in the Arabic language. The Arabic word for God is *Allah*. The Islamic name for God is Allah.

This is a mosque in the Malaysian capital city of Kuala Lumpur. Muslims worship on Fridays at mosques.

Every year more than two million Muslims make the pilgrimage to Mecca to worship and to pray.

Island

see also: Coast, Coral, Ocean

An island is an area of land with water all around it. An island can be in a lake, a sea, or an ocean. It can be very large or very small. Greenland is the largest island in the world.

DID YOU KNOW?

Some islands have plants and animals that do not live anywhere else in the world. This is because the sea separated them from other land.

How islands are made

Some islands are volcanoes that have pushed up from the bottom of the ocean. The Hawaiian Islands in the Pacific Ocean were made this way. Other islands have formed over thousands of years. They formed from living and dead sea animals called coral.

About ten thousand years ago lots of ice melted on Earth. Many areas of land were covered with water. Only the high parts of land were left out of the water. This is another way that many islands were made.

These small islands were once the high parts of a land area. The lighter blue shows where there is land very close to the surface of the water.

People and islands

Some islands are too small for anyone to live on. There is no drinking water. There is not enough land to grow crops. Islands in hot areas are often popular vacation spots. They have lots of coast. They are good for fishing, watersports, and watching wildlife.

This island is off the Alaskan coast. It was formed by a volcano that is still active.

Israel

see also: Asia

Israel is a country in the Middle East. It is mostly lowland. There are some mountains to the east and to the north. There is desert to the south. It is hot and dry in the summer. It is cooler and wetter in the winter.

Jerusalem is a very old city. Its history goes back about 5,000 years.

Living in Israel

Most people live in towns and cities. More than half of the land is used for farming and grazing for animals. Farmers use spraying and pipes to get water to their crops.

Israel became a country in 1948. Most of the people living in Israel are Jewish. Israel was formed out of part of the area called Palestine. Not everyone in Palestine wanted the new country. This has caused fighting and wars ever since 1948.

DID YOU KNOW?

Jerusalem is a holy city for Jews, Muslims, and Christians. Many people visit Israel for religious reasons.

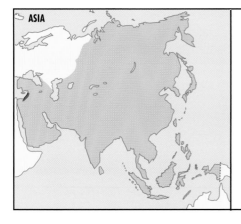

FACT FILE

PEOPLE...................... Israelis

POPULATION.............. about 6 million

MAIN LANGUAGES....... Hebrew, Arabic

CAPITAL CITY..............Jerusalem

MONEY......................Shekel

HIGHEST MOUNTAIN... Har Meron—3,965 feet

LONGEST RIVER..........Jordan River—200 miles

Italy

see also: Europe; Rome, Ancient

Italy is a country in south Europe. There are mountains in the north and center of Italy. The weather is hot and dry in the summer. It is mild and wet in the winter. There are active volcanoes in the south.

Living in Italy

Italian farmers grow grapes, olives, oranges, wheat, and tomatoes. Italian food is famous all over the world. Spaghetti and pizza are two of its well-known foods. Italy is also famous for its fashion clothing. Big fashion shows are held in cities like Milan.

Vatican City is in the city of Rome. It is the center of the government of the Roman Catholic Church. Many people visit St. Peter's Square in Vatican City.

This is the Leaning Tower of Pisa. Scientists hope to support its foundation so it will not lean any further.

DID YOU KNOW?

Tourists visit Italy to see the old buildings and works of art. Many tourists visit the Italian city of Venice. Venice is built on islands. It has water canals instead of roads.

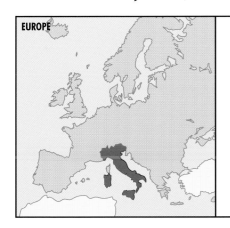

FACT FILE

PEOPLE	Italians
POPULATION	about 57 million
MAIN LANGUAGE	Italian
CAPITAL CITY	Rome
MONEY	Euro
HIGHEST MOUNTAIN	Monte Rosa—15,209 feet
LONGEST RIVER	Po River—404 miles

Jaguar

see also: Cat, Leopard

The jaguar is a mammal. It is a member of the cat family. Jaguars live in Central and South America. Jaguars look a lot like leopards, but jaguars are heavier and stronger. Jaguars also have bigger spots than leopards. The jaguar can climb trees and swim.

JAGUAR FACTS

NUMBER OF KINDS.....	8
COLOR	yellow with beige and black spots, or totally black
LENGTH	up to 70 inches
HEIGHT.......	up to 30 inches
WEIGHT......	up to 240 lbs.
STATUS	endangered
LIFE SPAN	about 20 years
ENEMIES	snakes, people

Jaguar families

Male and female jaguars live apart. Baby jaguars are called cubs. The female has her cubs in a safe den. She has from one to four cubs at a time. The cubs leave when they are six months old. Then they hunt on their own.

spotted coat to hide in forest shadows

strong teeth to kill and eat food

long tail to balance when climbing

sharp claws for climbing and fighting

soft paws to walk very quietly

a jaguar

MEAT EATER

A jaguar does not need to run far to find food. It hunts by creeping up on animals. It eats big animals such as tapir or deer. It eats small animals such as mice.

This jaguar cub is playing on a fallen tree.

Jamaica

see also: North America

Jamaica is an island country in the Caribbean Sea. Most of Jamaica is covered with mountains and streams. There are lowlands on the south coast. The climate is tropical. It is hot all year round. The climate is cooler in the mountains.

Living in Jamaica

About half of all Jamaicans live in rural areas. Many people work with the tourists who vacation in Jamaica.

Sugar cane, bananas, coffee, coconuts, and oranges are grown on farms and plantations. These crops are sold to other countries. Farmers also grow beans, rice, and fruit for local people. Fishermen sell fish to hotels and restaurants.

Music is very popular in Jamaica. Jamaica's reggae music is popular all over the world.

Reggae music began in Jamaica. It developed from a traditional form of Jamaican folk music called mento.

DID YOU KNOW?

The first people who lived on Jamaica were the Arawak Indians. They named the island *Xaymaca*. This means "the land of wood and water."

NORTH AMERICA

FACT FILE

PEOPLE	Jamaicans
POPULATION	about 2 million
MAIN LANGUAGES	English, Jamaican Creole
CAPITAL CITY	Kingston
MONEY	Jamaican dollar
HIGHEST MOUNTAIN	Blue Mountain Peak–7,404 feet
LONGEST RIVER	Black River–44 miles

Japan

see also: Asia, Earthquake

Japan is a country in southeast Asia. Japan is made up of four large islands and many smaller islands. There are volcanic mountains in the middle of the islands. There are lowlands around the coasts. The north is cold. The south is hot. It rains a lot in Japan.

Living in Japan

Most people in Japan live in the cities. Japan has many factories. Radios, stereos, and televisions are made in Japan. Japan makes more electrical goods than any other country. Japanese-made ships and cars are sold all over the world. Farmers grow rice and fruit. Fishing is also important. Rice and fish are often eaten with soy or spicy sauces.

The Japanese follow many customs from the country's past. There is a special ceremony for serving tea. There are also rules about how people should greet each other.

DID YOU KNOW?

Earthquakes are common in Japan. There was a very big earthquake in the city of Kobe in 1995. More than 5,000 people were killed.

Tokyo is the world's most expensive city in which to live.

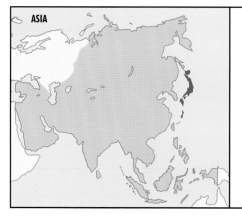

ASIA

FACT FILE

PEOPLE	Japanese
POPULATION	about 125 million
MAIN LANGUAGE	Japanese
CAPITAL CITY	Tokyo
MONEY	Yen
HIGHEST MOUNTAIN	Mount Fuji—12,393 feet
LONGEST RIVER	Shinano—228 miles

Jazz

see also: Music, Musical Instruments

Jazz is a form of music. Jazz was started by African Americans about 100 years ago. Jazz is made up of rhythm and improvisation. Improvisation is when jazz musicians make changes in the music while they are playing. Each performance of the same tune can be different.

Today's jazz bands might use the same instruments as a pop music band.

Traditional and modern jazz

Early jazz is now called traditional jazz. It is usually played by a small group of musicians. They play drums, bass, and piano. Sometimes they also play wind or brass instruments, such as clarinet, trumpet, or trombone. A banjo might used to play chords. There might be a singer, too.

There are many kinds of modern jazz today. Other places in the world, such as Latin America and Africa, now have their own styles of jazz.

DID YOU KNOW?

The word "cool" is used today to mean something that you like. The word comes from a modern kind of jazz. It is called "cool jazz."

Louis Armstrong (1900–1971)

Louis Armstrong was born in New Orleans, Louisiana. He played the trumpet, piano, and cornet. He also sang. Armstrong had many exciting ideas about how to change tunes as he played. He also used his voice like an instrument. He would sing sounds instead of words. This is called *scat* singing.

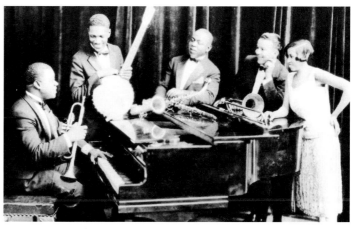

Louis Armstrong is sitting at a piano with one of his early groups called The Hot Five.

Jellyfish

see also: Invertebrate, Sea Life

A jellyfish is an invertebrate. It is made mostly of soft, jellylike flesh. A jellyfish is shaped like a bell. They are found in all the seas of the world.

Jellyfish families

A jellyfish develops from an egg. It hatches into a polyp. The polyp sticks to the sea bottom. It produces buds. The buds hatch into tiny jellyfish. These tiny jellyfish grow into large, adult jellyfish.

PLANT AND MEAT EATER

Most jellyfish eat plankton. Plankton is made up of tiny plants and animals that float in the sea.

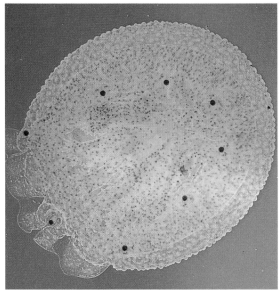

This is a jellyfish polyp. It is in the ocean near the Great Barrier Reef in Australia.

JELLYFISH FACTS

NUMBER OF KINDS	200
COLOR	clear, pink, orange, blue, or other colors
LENGTH	less than an inch to 7 feet
STATUS	common
LIFE SPAN	usually 1 to 3 months
ENEMIES	fish and other sea animals

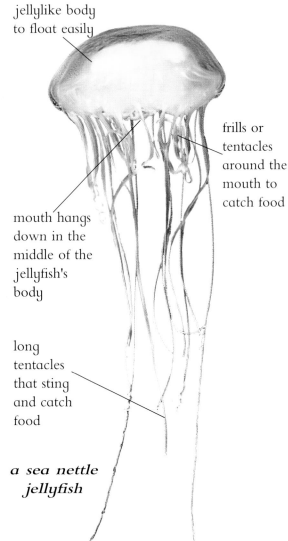

jellylike body to float easily

frills or tentacles around the mouth to catch food

mouth hangs down in the middle of the jellyfish's body

long tentacles that sting and catch food

a sea nettle jellyfish

Jordan

see also: Asia

Jordan is a country in the Middle East. Most of the land is flat desert. There is a river valley in the west. There are mountains in the south. The summer is very hot. The winter is cool with some rain.

Living in Jordan

Most Jordanians live in cities and towns. Only a small amount of the land is good for farming. Some grains, olives, figs, almonds, grapes, apricots, cucumbers, and tomatoes are grown. Some of the fruits and vegetables are sold to other countries.

Tribes called the *Bedouin* live in the deserts. They live in black tents. The Bedouin are nomads. They move from place to place with everything they own.

Jordanians are mostly Arabs. They follow the religion of Islam. Many of their customs and festivals are part of their religion.

These people are wearing traditional clothes. Their headdresses protect them from the sun and blowing sand.

DID YOU KNOW?

The Dead Sea is part of Jordan's border with Israel. The Dead Sea is really a big lake. It is nine times more salty than most oceans. It is easy to float in the Dead Sea.

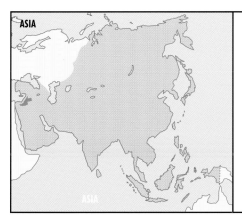

ASIA

FACT FILE

PEOPLE...................... Jordanians

POPULATION............... 4.5 million

MAIN LANGUAGE......... Arabic

CAPITAL CITY.............. Amman

MONEY....................... Jordanian dinar

HIGHEST MOUNTAIN... Jabal Ramm–4,923 feet

LONGEST RIVER........... Jordan River–200 miles

Judaism

see also: Israel, World War Two

Judaism is a world religion. Its followers are called Jews. The religion started from the belief in one God. It began in what is now Israel more than 3,000 years ago.

Beliefs and teachings

Jews believe that God gave laws called the Ten Commandments to Moses. Moses was a leader of the people of Israel. The Ten Commandments tell people how they should live.

One of the most important Jewish holy books is the Torah. It is written in Hebrew. A Jewish religious leader is called a *rabbi*.

This is the Western Wall in the city of Jerusalem. The wall is all that is left of an old Jewish temple.

Judaism today

There are now about 16 million Jews. Most live in the U.S.A., Israel, Britain, and Russia. Six million Jews were killed in Europe during the 1930s and during World War II. The terrible treatment and murder of Jews during this time is called the *Holocaust*.

DID YOU KNOW?

Israel was founded in 1948 as a country for Jews. Most of the holy places named in the Torah are in Israel.

A Jewish wedding ceremony is held under a special, decorated canopy.

Kangaroo

see also: Australia, Mammal, Marsupial

A kangaroo is a large marsupial mammal. *Marsupial* means that the female has a pouch. This is where she carries her baby. Kangaroos live in Australia. They also live on islands near Australia.

Kangaroo families

A young kangaroo is called a joey. The joey is tiny when it is born. It crawls up the mother's fur. It goes into her pouch. The joey stays in the pouch until it is about eight months old. Female kangaroos and their joeys live in groups. The groups are called herds.

long tail for balancing when jumping, standing, or walking —

This newborn joey is in its mother's pouch. It will drink its mother's milk.

KANGAROO FACTS

NUMBER OF	
KINDS	about 50
COLOR	usually brown or gray
LENGTH	2 feet to 10 feet
HEIGHT	up to 7 feet
WEIGHT	up to 155 lbs.
STATUS	common
LIFE SPAN	up to 15 years
ENEMIES	wedgetail eagles, dingoes, people

a female kangaroo and her joey

large ears turn to catch sounds

long back legs to jump as far as 43 feet

female's pouch shelters and protects the joey until the joey is too big to get in and out

PLANT EATER

A kangaroo eats in the early morning and the early evening during hot weather. It eats grass, leaves, and bark. A kangaroo rests during the day in the shade of a tree.

Kenya

see also: Africa

Kenya is a country in East Africa. There are hot lowlands and coastal areas in the east. There is higher land with mountains in the west. The Rift Valley runs through Kenya from north to south. The north is hot desert. The rainy season is in April and May.

Living in Kenya

Most Kenyans live in the rural areas. They work on farms. They raise animals. They grow food to eat. Coffee and tea are grown on big farms. These two crops are sold to other countries.

The people come from 40 African tribes. The national motto is *Harambee*. This means "Let's all pull together."

These men of the Samburu tribe are performing a traditional war dance.

DID YOU KNOW?

Many wild animals roam in Kenya's national parks. Tourists go on "camera safaris." The tourists travel through the parks and take photographs of the animals.

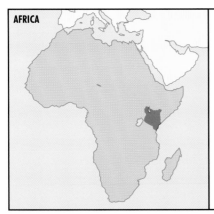

AFRICA

FACT FILE

PEOPLE	Kenyans
POPULATION	about 27 million
MAIN LANGUAGES	Swahili, English
CAPITAL CITY	Nairobi
MONEY	Kenyan shilling
HIGHEST MOUNTAIN	Mount Kenya—17,063 feet
LONGEST RIVER	Tana River—453 miles

Kiwi

see also: Bird, New Zealand

A kiwi is a bird that cannot fly. It lives only in New Zealand. A kiwi can run fast. It has feathers that look like hairs.

Kiwi families

The female kiwi lays two eggs. She lays them in a nest hole or in a hollow log. The male sits on the eggs for eleven weeks. This is longer than any other bird sits on eggs. The young kiwi are called chicks. The chicks have all their feathers when they hatch. They can see, too. The chicks leave the nest after one week. They go off on their own.

KIWI FACTS

NUMBER OF KINDS	3
COLOR	brownish-gray
HEIGHT	14 inches
LENGTH	20 inches
WEIGHT	up to 5 lbs.
STATUS	common
LIFE SPAN	not known
ENEMIES	rats, stoats, ferrets

a common kiwi

long beak for reaching worms

sensitive nostrils for smelling food

strong legs for running and kicking in fights

PLANT, INSECT, AND MEAT EATER

A kiwi sleeps in the daytime. It walks around at night looking for insects, worms, berries, fruit, and lizards to eat.

This female brown kiwi has just laid this egg. The egg is very large compared to her size.

Knight

see also: Middle Ages

A knight was a fighting man. He fought while riding a horse. This was in Europe in the Middle Ages. Knights fought for a king or queen. They also fought for the most important person where they lived.

What did a knight wear?
Knights wore armor to fight. Armor was made from pieces of metal. The metal was shaped to fit different parts of the body. It was difficult to hurt a knight when he was covered from head to foot in metal. Armor was very heavy. Knights could not move fast. Their horses had to be very strong.

A knight fought with a lance. A lance is a long pole with sharp metal on the end. Knights also had swords and daggers.

Who could be a knight?
Knights were men from important families. Boys lived in a knight's home. The boys worked as pages. The pages fetched and carried things for the knight. They served his food. A page became a squire when he was older. Squires trained to be knights. Then they became knights in a special ceremony.

Knights were not needed for fighting any more after about A.D. 1600.

Armor had many parts. These pictures show the layers of clothes a knight needed to put on.

Koala

see also: Australia, Mammal, Marsupial

A koala is a marsupial mammal. Marsupial means that the female has a pouch for her young. Koalas look like small bears. They live only in Australia. A koala lives most of its life in the trees. It can walk or swing from tree to tree. A koala never drinks. It gets all the water it needs when it eats eucalyptus leaves.

Koala families

A newborn koala is less than one inch long. It is blind and hairless. It climbs through its mother's fur to her pouch. It drinks her milk while it is in the pouch. The baby is six months old when it leaves the pouch. Then it moves onto its mother's back.

A female koala carries her baby on her back until it is fully grown.

KOALA FACTS

NUMBER OF KINDS	1
COLOR	gray and white
LENGTH	up to 30 inches
WEIGHT	up to 26 lbs.
STATUS	common
LIFE SPAN	about 15 to 20 years
ENEMIES	people who destroy eucalyptus forests

long fingers and strong claws for climbing trees

thick fur for keeping warm at night

a koala

PLANT EATER

A koala is a very fussy eater. The only food it eats is the leaves from twelve kinds of eucalyptus tree. A koala feeds at night. It moves from one tree to another to find enough leaves to eat.

Kuwait

see also: Asia, Desert

Kuwait is a country in the Middle East. It is all flat lowland. Kuwait has a coast in the east. It is mostly very hot desert. It is a bit cooler from October to March. There is very little rain.

Living in Kuwait

Nearly everybody in Kuwait lives in cities or towns. Kuwait City is very modern. It has lots of tall buildings. The only big industry is the production of oil and natural gas. There are thousands of oil wells.

No food can be grown in Kuwait. Shrimp and fish are caught in the sea. All other food is bought from other countries. Drinking water is made by taking the salt out of the sea water. This is called *desalination*. It is done in special factories.

These men are building a **dhow**. *A* **dhow** *is a traditional Arab sailboat.*

DID YOU KNOW?

Kuwait is one of the Gulf States. This is the name given to all the countries that are around the Persian Gulf.

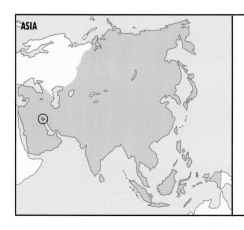

ASIA

FACT FILE

PEOPLE........................ Kuwaitis

POPULATION .... about 2 million

MAIN LANGUAGE......... Arabic

CAPITAL CITY.............. Kuwait

MONEY....................... Kuwaiti dinar

HIGHEST MOUNTAIN... no land above 650 feet

LONGEST RIVER........... no rivers

Ladybug

see also: Beetle, Insect

A ladybug is a brightly-colored, spotted beetle. They are found in most parts of the world, but not in very cold places. Ladybugs are also called ladybirds.

Ladybug families

A ladybird egg hatches into a larva. The larva is a gray grub. It has black, red, blue, or green spots. A fully grown larva spins a special covering. It forms a pupa. Inside the pupa, it changes into an adult ladybug.

LADYBUG FACTS

NUMBER OF	
KINDS	5,000
COLOR	brightly colored with black, yellow, or red spots
LENGTH	less than one inch
STATUS	common
LIFE SPAN	less than a year
ENEMIES	birds, chemical pesticides

different kinds of ladybugs have different numbers and colors of spots

a ladybug

hard covers to protect the wings underneath

INSECT EATER

A ladybug is a friend to gardeners and farmers. It eats greenflies and other insects that damage plants.

These young ladybugs are gathering together in a swarm.

Lake

see also: River, Valley

A lake is an area of water. It has land all around it. Some lakes are so big that they are called seas. A very small lake is called a pond.

How lakes are made

There are two ways many lakes have formed. One way is from the ice that covered the earth a long, long time ago. Sheets of ice dug deep holes in the ground. Lakes formed in these holes. Another way lakes have formed is from cracks in the earth's surface. These cracks are called fault lines. The cracks can fill up with water to make a lake.

There is fresh water in most lakes. Fresh water rivers sometimes flow into lakes. Then the rivers flow out again. Some lakes are very salty. This is because rivers that flow into the lake are carrying salt from rocks.

People and lakes

Large boats on lakes carry goods. People also make special lakes to store water. These lakes are called *reservoirs.* People use lakes for fishing, boating, and water sports. Lakes are also important homes for wildlife.

The Great Salt Lake in Utah is very salty. Salty rivers flow into it.

DID YOU KNOW?

The deepest lakes in Africa are along a huge fault line called the Great Rift Valley. Water filled the hollows along the crack where the land sank. This made the lakes.

Loch Ness in Scotland is a lake formed along a fault line. It is famous for the Loch Ness monster that some people believe lives there.

Language

see also: Alphabet, Communication

Language is how people communicate with each other. People use language to tell others what they want, think, or feel. Language is both spoken words and written words. Today, there are about 6,000 languages in the world.

Language around the world

More people speak Chinese than any other language. Many people speak English, Hindi, Spanish, French, Russian, and Arabic. There are about 1,300 languages in Africa. All of them probably started from just four languages. Languages change over time.

English

The English language began to spread around the world about 400 years ago. People traveled to new places. They spread their language as they traveled. Now more than 320 million people speak English. Many people also learn English as their second language.

Chinese Japanese	魚
Dutch	VIS
Spanish	PEZ
Greek	ΨΑΡΙ
Russian	РЫБА
Finnish	KALA
Swedish	FISK
English	FISH
German	FISCH
Italian	PESCE
French	POISSON
Turkish	BALIK

Here is the word fish in twelve languages. This word is nearly the same in some languages. In other languages, the word looks very different.

This teacher uses sign language to read a story to children who are deaf.

DID YOU KNOW?

Sign language is a special way to communicate. People use their hands to make symbols or spell out words in this language. Sign language was invented for people who cannot hear or speak.

Laser

see also: Bar Code, Computer, Light

A laser is a machine. It makes a ray of light. Lasers have many uses. Tiny lasers are used in CD players and cable TV. Powerful lasers are used in medical operations.

DID YOU KNOW?

A hologram is a photograph or image. It is made using lasers. Two laser beams shine on an object from different directions. This makes views of the object from different sides. The finished hologram shows the different sides.

How do lasers work?

All beams of light carry energy. All of the energy in a laser light is in a very narrow beam. The beam makes a a tiny spot. This tiny spot is very hot in a powerful laser.

How is a laser used?

Some laser beams carry TV and radio signals. Other carry telephone messages. Many signals can be sent a long way through cables.

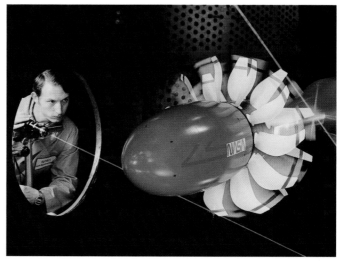

The red lines are laser beams. Laser beams stay narrow. Regular light spreads out.

CD players use laser beams. The beam shines on the CD and bounces off it. This light is the code for the music. Nothing touches the disc. The disc does not wear out. Doctors use lasers like knives to cut during operations. Laser beams can also burn away tumors.

This laser machine is held by a robot arm. The arm moves and shoots out laser beams. The beams make a clean cut through metal.

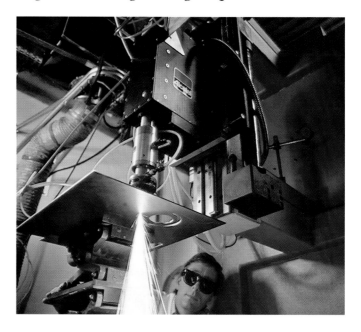

Leaf

see also: Photosynthesis, Plants

A leaf is part of a plant. It makes the plant's food. Green plants grow almost everywhere except where it is very cold or very dry. Different plants have different shaped leaves.

Life of a leaf

A bud forms on the stem of a plant. The bud opens. A new leaf and stem begin to grow. The leaves of some plants live for years. The leaves of many other plants die after several months.

People and animals could not live without leaves. Many animals eat leaves, grass, and plants. Meat eaters eat the plant-eating animals. People eat the leaves of some plants. Some leaves are used as medicines. Tea is made from the leaves of tea plants.

narrow tube-like veins carry water to the leaf and take food away from the leaf

chlorophyll gives the leaf its green color and turns light into food

stem joins the leaf to the rest of the plant

The African raffia palm has the largest leaves of any tree. The leaves grow up to 65 feet long.

DID YOU KNOW?

Some leaves change color in the autumn. Then they fall off the trees and plants. This is because the water supply to the leaves has stopped. Then the green chlorophyll stops forming and other colors appear.

Lebanon

see also: Asia

Lebanon is a country in the Middle East. It has two mountain ranges. There is good farm land between the mountain ranges. There is a narrow coast in the west. Summers are hot. Winters are cool. Lebanon gets some rain.

Living in Lebanon

Most Lebanese live in the cities and towns. There is some industry. Things are made from chemicals, gold, and silver. Farmers grow fruits, olives, grapes, and tobacco. Olives are a favorite snack in Lebanon.

People have lived in Lebanon for thousands of years. In recent times, Lebanon has had about 50 years of war. There has been fighting between Arabs, Palestinians, and Israelis.

Beirut has a natural harbor. It has been used by ships for thousands of years.

DID YOU KNOW?

The tree called the Cedar of Lebanon has been a symbol of Lebanon for about 2,000 years. The tree symbol is on Lebanon's flag. Some Cedars of Lebanon are more than 3,000 years old.

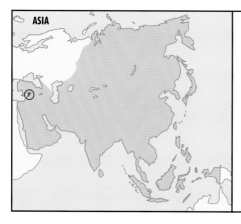

ASIA

FACT FILE

PEOPLE...................... Lebanese

POPULATION............... about 3 million

MAIN LANGUAGES....... Arabic, French

CAPITAL CITY.............. Beirut

MONEY...................... Lebanese pound

HIGHEST MOUNTAIN... Qurnat as Sawdā'—10,135 feet

LONGEST RIVER.......... Litani River—90 miles

Legend

see also: Literature, Myth, Story

A legend is a story that has been handed down through the years. The story is often about heroes or exciting events. Legends can have magic or supernatural things in them, but the stories are always about human beings. This makes legends different from myths. Myths are about gods or supernatural beings. Every country in the world has its own legends.

Real and pretend

Many legends are based on real people. The English legends of King Arthur may be about a real person. The legends say that King Arthur had a magic sword. They say he had a magician called Merlin. The legends also say that King Arthur and his knights sat around a round table. Some of these things may be true. Some of these things may be pretend. Pieces are added to legends as the stories are told again and again.

JOHNNY APPLESEED

Johnny Appleseed was the nickname of a real person. His name was John Chapman. He was an early American settler in the 1800s. He planted apple trees, so people called him Appleseed. Many of the stories about him and his family are pretend.

Johnny Appleseed is a hero in American legends.

This picture is 600 years old. It shows King Arthur and his knights.

Leopard

see also: Cat, Mammal, Jaguar

The leopard is a mammal. It is a member of the cat family. Leopards live in Africa and southern Asia. Most leopards live on grassy plains. Leopards also live in very hot areas and in high mountains.

LEOPARD FACTS

NUMBER OF KINDS....	7
COLOR......	yellow with black and brown spots, or totally black
LENGTH.....	up to 6 feet
HEIGHT.....	up to 28 inches
WEIGHT.....	up to 200 lbs.
STATUS......	endangered
LIFE SPAN...	about 12 years
ENEMIES.....	people

long tail for balance

spotted coat for hiding

soft paws for walking very quietly

the leopard

strong teeth for killing and eating food

sharp claws for climbing and fighting

Leopard families

Adult leopards live by themselves. The female makes a home called a lair. This is where she has her babies. The babies are called cubs. The mother moves her lair every few days to keep her young cubs safe. The cubs stay with their mother for about two years.

MEAT EATER

A leopard catches antelopes, baboons, and warthogs. It will also eat smaller animals and birds. The leopard carries its food up into trees. This keeps its food out of the reach of lions and vultures.

A female leopard cares for her cub.